Meag[...]

Th[...]

All Things Are

Possible!

♡ Patty

15/16

To:

_____

From:

_____

Tweets for My Friend

© 2013 Christian Art Gifts, RSA
Christian Art Gifts Inc., IL, USA

Designed by Christian Art Gifts

Images used under license from Shutterstock.com

Scripture quotations are taken from the *Holy Bible*,
New International Version® NIV®. Copyright © 1973, 1978, 1984
by International Bible Society. Used by permission of
Zondervan Publishing House. All rights reserved.

Scripture quotations are taken from the *Holy Bible*, New Living Translation®,
second edition. Copyright © 1996, 2004 by Tyndale House Publishers, Inc.,
Carol Stream, Illinois 60188.
All rights reserved.

Scripture quotations are taken from the
Contemporary English Version®.
Copyright © 1995 by American Bible Society.
All rights reserved.

Scripture quotations are taken from *The Message*.
Copyright © by Eugene H. Peterson, 1993, 1994, 1995,
1996, 2000, 2001, 2002 by NavPress Publishing Group.
Used by permission.

Printed in China

ISBN 978-1-4321-0694-2

Christian Art Gifts has made every effort to trace the ownership of all quotes
and poems in this book. In the event of any question that may arise from
the use of any quote or poem, we regret any error made and will be pleased
to make the necessary correction in future editions of this book.

© All rights reserved. No part of this book may be reproduced in any form
without permission in writing from the publisher, except in the case of brief
quotations embodied in critical articles or reviews.

13 14 15 16 17 18 19 20 21 22 – 10 9 8 7 6 5 4 3 2 1

Tweets
for
My Friend

christian art gifts®

A friend
in your life
is a joy in
your heart.

#Let'sTweetupSoon!

Life is beautiful!

Especially when you're with me.

God gives only the
best gifts.
That's why He
blessed me
with you!

#SoBlessed

It's not where you are in life, it's who you have by your side that matters.

A hug is worth a thousand words.

A friend is worth more.

#UR Priceless

He who sows courtesy reaps friendship, and he who plants kindness gathers love.

@StBasil

You are truly a #gift_from_God!

May you experience the love of Christ.

@Ephesians3:19

So long as the memory of certain beloved friends lives in my heart, I shall say that #life_is_good.

@HelenKeller

May your joys be
as deep as
the ocean,
your sorrows
as light as its foam.

The joy of the LORD is your strength.

@Nehemiah8:10

Friends are flowers

in the #garden_of_life.

#UR Beautiful

Grace
and peace
be yours in
abundance.

@2Peter1:2

Great friends
are hard to find,
difficult to leave,
impossible to forget.

#1UnforgettableFriend

You have a special place in my heart.

@Philippians1:7

You are the best friend ever!

Today's forecast:

#God_reigns
and the
#Son_shines!

#HelloSunshine

God's love
and kindness
will shine
upon us

like the sun that
rises in the sky.

@Luke1:78

Perfume and incense bring joy to the heart, and the pleasantness of a friend springs from their heartfelt advice.

@Proverbs27:9

The Lord bless you and keep you.

@Numbers6:24

The Lord
will guide you
always.

@Isaiah58:11

May the God of hope fill you with all joy and peace.

@Romans15:13

From the
fullness of

His grace

we have all received

one blessing
after another.

@John1:16

I count my blessings every day, starting with you!

#SoThankfulForYou

Friendship is a plant
we must often water.

@Proverb

A single rose can
be my garden ...
a single friend,

my world.

@LeoBuscaglia

The blessings
of our
friendship
are as numerous
as the stars in the sky

#URaStar

#Friends

are those rare people who ask how you are and then wait for the answer.

#LoveChattingToU

You are precious to God and He loves you.

@Isaiah43:4

#Friendship is a sheltering tree.

@SamuelTaylorColeridge

A friend may well be reckoned the masterpiece of nature.

@RalphWaldoEmerson

Two people are better off than one,
for they can help each other succeed.
@Ecclesiastes4:9

There is no greater treasure than the respect and love of a true friend.

Who finds a faithful friend, finds a treasure.

#ULittleGem

Every
time
I think of you,
I give thanks
to my God.
@Philippians1:3

Thank you

for always making me

smile!

:D :D :)

A friend is some-
one who knows the
#songinyourheart
and sings it back
to you when you
have forgotten
how it goes.

Friendship is a treasured gift,

and every time I talk with you I feel as if I'm getting richer and richer.

@YourBlessedFriend

When I'm with you,
silences are
never awkward.

These
three remain:
faith, hope
and love.
But the greatest
of these is
love.

@1Corinthians13:13

A friend
is one who
knows all about you
and
loves you
just the same.

@ElbertHubbard

Thank you
for all the times you make me laugh!

#LOLwithU

You sprinkle my world with JOY!

#Life_is_sweet

Your
friendship
is priceless.

@YourFriend

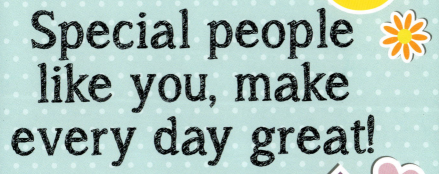

Special people like you, make every day great!

#URAwesome

Our love to God is measured by our everyday fellowship with others and the love it displays.

@AndrewMurray

In my
heart,
I'm holding you
tight.

#HugTime

A friend

is someone who understands your past, believes in your future, and accepts you just the way you are.

#Accepted&Loved

Friends make life

So tweet!

#USweetiePie

#Friendship

is the only cement that will
ever hold the world together.

@WoodrowWilson

Always remember:

you're precious and loved.

There is nothing on this earth more to be prized than

true friendship.

@ThomasAquinas

Friendship is one of the *sweetest joys of life.*

@Charles Spurgeon

Friends
are God's way
of taking
care of us.

#TakenCareOf

Wherever we
are, it is our
friends
that make our

world.

@HenryDrummond

Friends **love** through all kinds of weather.

@Proverbs17:17

I never stop being #grateful_for_you, as I mention you in my prayers.

@Ephesians1:16

Love each other with genuine affection,
and take delight in honoring each other.
@Romans12:10

I have learned that to have a good friend is the purest of all God's gifts, for it is a love that has no exchange of payment.

@FrancesFarmer

May our **Lord Jesus Christ** Himself #encourageyourhearts and strengthen you in every good deed and word.

@2Thessalonians2:16-17

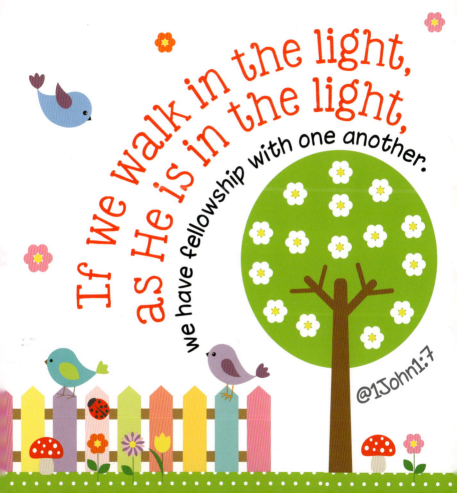

If we walk in the light, as He is in the light, we have fellowship with one another.

@1John1:7

Laughter is not a bad beginning for a friendship, and it is the best ending for one.

@HenryWardBeecher

May the Lord keep
watch between you and
me when we are away
from each other.

@Genesis31:49

I wouldn't trade you
for anything in the world!
You're irreplaceable!

#UR1inaMillion

No matter where we
are, I always enjoy the
gift of your company.

Friendships
are discovered
rather than made.

@HarrietBeecherStowe

Friendships
begun in
this world
will be
taken up again,
never to be
broken off.

@FrancisdeSales

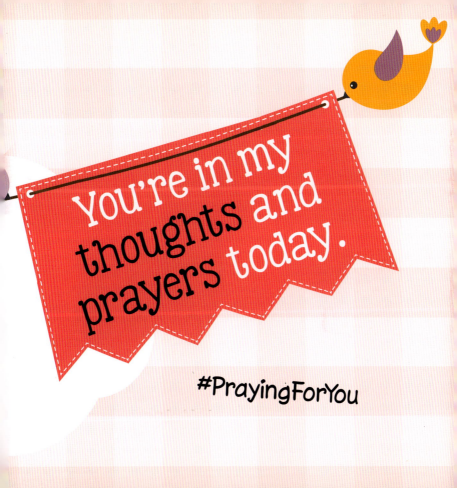

You're in my thoughts and prayers today.

#PrayingForYou

The LORD offers His **friendship** to the godly.

@Proverbs3:32

How rare and wonderful is that flash of a moment when we realize we have discovered a friend.

@WilliamRotsler

Human fellowship can go to great lengths, but not all the way. Fellowship with God can go to all lengths.

@OswaldChambers

Prayer is nothing else than being on terms of friendship with God.

@StTeresaofAvila

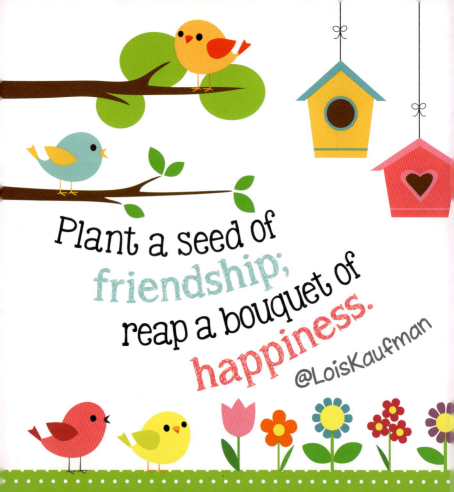

Plant a seed of friendship; reap a bouquet of happiness.

@LoisKaufman